Trustful Surrender

to

Divine Providence

The Secret of Peace and Happiness

by

Fr. Jean Baptiste Saint-Jure

&

St. Claude de la Colombiere

Table *of* Contents

Part I

by Father Jean Baptiste Saint-Jure

I

The Will *of* God Made *and* Governs All Things

1. God controls all events, whether good or bad
   How can God will or allow evil?
   Practical examples

2. God does everything with supreme wisdom
   Trials and punishments are blessings from God and proof of His mercy
   Our trials are never greater than our strength to bear them

Treating of the Will of God St. Thomas, following St. Augustine, teaches that it is the cause of all that exists.[1] The Psalmist tells us that "all that the Lord wills he does in heaven and on earth, in the seas and in all the deeps."[2] Again in the Book of the Apocalypse it is written: "Worthy art thou, O Lord our God, to receive glory and honor and power; for thou hast created all things, and because of *thy will* they existed and were created.[3]

Hence it is the Will of God which from nothingness drew out the universe with all its grandeur and all that lives in it, the earth with all that is on it and beneath it, all creatures visible and invisible, living and inanimate, reasonable and without reason, from the highest to the lowest.

If God then has produced all these things, as St. Paul says, *according to the purpose of his will,*[4] is it not supremely right and reasonable as well as absolutely necessary that they should be preserved and governed by Him according to the counsel of His will? And how could a thing remain, unless you willed it; or be preserved, had it not been called forth by you?[5]

---

[1] *St. Thomas, Sum. p. 1, q. 19, a. 4;*
St. Augustine, De Gen.
[2] *Ps. 134:6*

[3] *Apoc. 4:11*
[4] *Eph. 1:5*
[5] *Wis. 11:25*

But the works of God are perfect it is written in the Canticle of Moses.[6] They are so well done that God Himself, whose judgment is strict and righteous, found when He had created them that they were *good and very good.*[7] It is quite obvious *that He who hath founded the earth by wisdom and hath established the heavens by understanding*[8] could not show less perfection in governing His works than in creating them. So, as He is careful to remind us, if his Providence continues *to have care of all things,*[9] it is *in measure and number and weight,*[10] it is *with justice and mercy.*[11] *Neither can any man say to him, Why dost thou so?*[12] For if He assigns to His creatures the end that He wills, and chooses the means which seem good to Him to lead them to it, the end He assigns them must be good and wise, nor can He direct them towards their end other than by good and wise means. *Therefore, do not become foolish*[13] the Apostle tells us, *but understand what the will of the Lord is, so that doing it you may receive the promise,*[14] that is to say eternal happiness, for it is written *the world with its lust is passing away, but he who does the will of God abides forever.*[15]

1. God Controls All Events, Whether Good *or* Bad

Nothing happens in the universe without God willing and allowing it. This statement must be taken absolutely of everything with the exception of sin. 'Nothing occurs by chance in the whole course of our lives' is the unanimous teaching of the Fathers and Doctors of the Church, 'and God intervenes everywhere.'

I am the Lord, He tells us Himself by the mouth of the prophet Isaias, *and there is none else. I form light and create darkness; I make peace and create evil. I, the Lord, do all these things.*[16] *It is I who bring both death and life, I who inflict wounds and heal them,* He said to Moses.[17] 'The Lord killeth and maketh alive, it is written in the Canticle of Anna, the mother of Samuel, *He bringeth down to the tomb and He bringeth back again; the Lord maketh poor and maketh rich, he humbleth and he exalteth.*[18] *Shall there be evil* (disaster, affliction) *in a city which the Lord hath not done?*[19] asks

---

[6] *Deut. 32:4*
[7] *Gen. 1:31*
[8] *Prov. 3:19*
[9] *Wis. 12:13*
[10] *id. 11:20*
[11] *id. 12:15; 16:1*
[12] *Eccles. 8:4*

[13] *Eph. 5:7*
[14] *Heb. 10:36*
[15] *1 John 2:17*
[16] *Is. 45:6-7*
[17] *Deut. 32:39*
[18] *1 Kings 2:6-7*
[19] *Amos 3:6*

the prophet Amos: *Good things and evil, life and death, poverty and riches are from God Solomon proclaims.*[20]

And so on in numerous other passages of Scripture.

Perhaps you will say that while this is true of certain necessary effects, like sickness, death, cold and heat, and other accidents due to natural causes which have no liberty of action, the same cannot be said in the case of things that result from the free will of man. For if, you will object, someone slanders me, robs me, strikes me, persecutes me, how can I attribute his conduct to the will of God who far from wishing me to be treated in such a manner, expressly forbids it? So the blame, you will conclude, can only be laid on the will of man, on his ignorance or malice. This is the defense behind which we try to shelter from God and excuse our lack of courage and submission.

It is quite useless for us to try and take advantage of this way of reasoning as an excuse for not surrendering to Providence. God Himself has refuted it and we must believe on His word that in events of this kind as in all others, nothing occurs except by His order and permission.

Let us see what the Scriptures say. He wishes to punish the murder and adultery committed by David and He expresses Himself as follows by the mouth of the prophet Nathan: *Why therefore hast thou despised the word of the Lord, to do evil in my sight? Thou hast killed Urias the Hittite with the sword, and hast taken his wife to be thy wife, and hast slain him with the sword of the children of Ammon. Therefore, the sword shall never depart from thy house, because thou hast despised me, and host taken the wife of Urias the Hittite to be thy wife. Thus saith the Lord: Behold, I will raise up evil against thee out of thy own house, and I will take thy wives before thy eyes and give them to thy neighbor and he shall lie with thy wives in the sight of this sun. For thou didst it secretly, but I will do this thing in the sight of all all Israel, and in the sight of the sun.*[21]

Later when the Jews by their iniquities had grievously offended Him and provoked His wrath, He says: *The Assyrian is the rod and the staff of my anger, and my indignation is in his hands. I will send him to the deceitful nation, and I will give him charge against the people of my wrath, to take away the spoils, and to lay hold on the prey, and to tread them down like the mire of the streets.*[22]

Could God more openly declare Himself to be responsible for the evils that Absalom caused his father and the King of Assyria the Jews? It

---

[20] *Ecclus. 11:14*

[21] *2 Kings 12:9-12*

[22] *Is. 10:5-6*

would be easy to find other instances but these are enough. Let us conclude then with St. Augustine: "All that happens to us in this world against our will (whether due to men or to other causes) happens to us only by the will of God, by the disposal of Providence, by His orders and under His guidance; and if from the frailty of our understanding we cannot grasp the reason for some event, let us attribute it to divine Providence, show Him respect by accepting it from His hand, believe firmly that He does not send it us without cause."

Replying to the murmurs and complaints of the Jews who attributed their captivity and sufferings to misfortune and causes other than the will of God, the prophet Jeremias says to them: *Who is he that hath commanded a thing to be done, when the Lord commandeth it not? Do not both evil and good proceed out of the mouth of the Highest? Why doth a living man murmur, a man suffering for his sins? Let us search our ways, and seek, and return to the Lord. Let us lift up our hearts with our hands to the Lord in the heavens, saying, We have done wickedly and provoked thee to wrath; therefore thou art inexorable.*[23]

Are not these words clear enough? We should take them to heart for our own good. Let us be careful to attribute everything to the will of God and believe that all is guided by His paternal hand.

How Can God Will *or* Allow Evil?

However, you will perhaps now say, there is sinfulness in all these actions. How then can God will them and take part in them if He is all-holy and can have nothing in common with sin?

God indeed is not and cannot be the author of sin. But it must be remembered that in every sin there are two parts to be distinguished, one natural and the other moral. Thus, in the action of the man you think you have a grievance against there is, for example, the movement of the arm that strikes you or the tongue that offends you, and the movement of the will that turns aside from right reason and the law of God. The physical action of the arm or the tongue, like all natural things, is quite good in itself and there is nothing to prevent its being produced with and by God's cooperation. What is evil, what God could not cooperate with, is the sinful intention which the will of man contributes to the act.

When a man walks with a crippled leg, the movement he makes comes both from the soul and the leg, but the defect which causes him to

---

[23] *Lam. 3:37-42*

walk badly is only in the leg. In the same way all evil actions must be attributed to God and to man in so far as they are natural, physical acts, but they can be attributed only to the will of man in so far as they are sinful and blameworthy.

If then someone strikes you or slanders you, as the movement of the arm or tongue is in no way a sin, God can very well be, and actually is, the author of it; for existence and movement in man not less than in any other creature proceed not from himself but from God, who acts in him and by him. *For in Him* says St. Paul, *we live and move and have our being.*[24] As for the malice of the intention, it proceeds entirely from man and in it alone is the sinfulness in which God has no share but which He yet permits in order not to interfere with our freedom of will.

Moreover, when God cooperates with the person who attacks or robs you, He doubtless intends to deprive you of health or goods because you are making a wrong use of them and they will be harmful to your soul. But He does not intend that the attacker or robber should take them from you by a sin. That is the part of human malice, not God's design.

An example may make the matter clearer. A criminal is condemned to death by fair trial. But the executioner happens to be a personal enemy of his, and instead of carrying out the judge's sentence as a duty, he does so in a spirit of hate and revenge. Obviously, the judge has no share in the executioner's sin. The will and intention of the judge is not that this sin should he committed, but that justice should take its course and the criminal be punished.

In the same way God has no share at all in the wickedness of the man who strikes or robs you. That is something particular to the man himself. God, as we have said, wishes to make you see your own faults, to humble you, deprive you of what you possess, in order to free you from vice and lead you to virtue; but this good and merciful design, which He could carry out in numerous other ways without any sin being involved, has nothing in common with the sin of the man who acts as His instrument. And in fact, it is not this man's evil intention or sin that causes you to suffer, humiliates or impoverishes you, but the loss of your well-being, your good name or your possessions. The sin harms only the person who is guilty of it. This is the way we ought to separate the good from the evil in events of this kind, and distinguish what God operates through men from what men add to the act by their own will.

---

[24] *Acts 17:28*

Practical Examples

St. Gregory sets the same truth before us in another light. A doctor, he says orders leeches to be applied. While these small creatures are drawing blood from the patient their only aim is to gorge themselves and suck up as much of it as they can. The doctor's only intention is to have the impure blood drawn from the patient and to cure him in this manner. There is therefore no relation between the insatiable greed of the leeches and the intelligent purpose of the doctor in using them. The patient himself does not protest at their use. He does not regard the leeches as evildoers. Rather he tries to overcome the repugnance the sight of their ugliness causes and help them in their action, in the knowledge that the doctor has judged it useful for his health.

God makes use of men as the doctor does of leeches. Neither should we then stop to consider the evilness of those to whom God gives power to act on us or be grieved at their wicked intentions, and we should keep ourselves from feelings of aversion towards them. Whatever their particular views may be, in regard to us they are only instruments of wellbeing, guided by the hand of an all-good, all-wise, all-powerful God who will allow them to act on us only in so far as is of use to us. It is in our interest to welcome instead of trying to repel their assaults, as in very truth they come from God. And it is the same with all creatures of whatever kind. Not one of them could act upon us unless the power were given it from above.

This truth has always been familiar to the minds of those truly enlightened by God. We have a celebrated example in Job. He loses his children and his possessions; he falls from the height of fortune to the depths of poverty. And he says *The Lord gave and the Lord hath taken away. As it hath pleased the Lord, so is it done. Blessed be the name of the Lord.*[25] "Note" observes St. Augustine "Job does not say 'The Lord gave and the devil hath taken away' but says, wise that he is, 'The Lord gave me my children and my possessions, and it is He who has taken them away; it has been done as it has pleased the Lord.'"

The example of Joseph is no less instructive. His brothers had sold him into slavery from malice and for a wicked purpose, and nevertheless the holy patriarch insists on attributing all to God's providence. *God sent me,* he says, *before you into Egypt to save life ... God sent me before you to preserve a remnant for you in the land, and to deliver you in striking way.*

---

[25] *Job 1:21*

10

Not you but God sent me here, and made me a father to Pharaoh, lord of all his house, and ruler over the land of Egypt.[26]

Let us now listen to Our Savior himself who came down from heaven to teach us by His word and example. In an excess of zeal Peter tries to turn him aside from His purpose of submitting to His passion and prevent the soldiers laying their hands on Him. But Jesus said to him: *Shall I not drink the cup that the Father has given me?*[27] In fact He attributed the suffering and ignominy of His passion not to the Jews who accused him, not to Judas who betrayed Him, nor to Pilate who condemned Him, nor to the soldiers who ill-treated and crucified Him, nor to the devil who incited them all, though they were the immediate causes of His sufferings, but to God, and to God not considered as a strict judge but as a loving and beloved Father.

Let us never then attribute our losses, our disappointments, our afflictions, our humiliations to the devil or to men, but to God as their real source. "To act otherwise" says St. Dorothy, "would be to do the same as a dog who vents his anger on the stone instead of putting the blame *on the hand that threw it at him*." So, let us be careful not to say 'So-and-so is the cause of my misfortune.' Your misfortunes are the work not of this or that person but of God. And what should give you reassurance is that God, the sovereign good, is guided in all His actions by His most profound wisdom for holy and supernatural purposes.

2. God Does Everything *with* Supreme Wisdom

All wisdom comes from the Lord God we find in the Book of Ecclesiasticus, and with him it remains forever, and is before all time ... and he has poured her forth upon all his works.[28] *How manifold are your works, O Lord!* exclaims the Psalmist, *In wisdom thou hast wrought them all*[29] It could not be otherwise, for God, being infinite wisdom and acting by Himself, cannot act except in an infinitely wise manner.

For this reason many of the Doctors of the Church hold that, having regard to the circumstances, His works are so perfect that they could not be more so, and so good that they could not be better. 'We ought then' says St. Basil, 'to ponder well on this thought, that we are the work of a good Workman, and that He dispenses and distributes to us all things great and small with the wisest providence, so that there is nothing had, nothing that could even be conceived better.' *The works of the Lord are*

---

[26] *Gen. 45:5-8*
[27] *John 18:11*

[28] *Eccles. 1:1,8*
[29] *Ps. 103:24*

great the Psalmist again says, *exquisite in all their delights.* [30] His wisdom is especially shown in the right proportion between the means He employs and the end He has in view. *She reaches from end to end mightily and governs all things well.* [31] She (Wisdom) governs men with admirable order, she leads them to their happiness mightily but without violence or constraint, with sweetness and not only with sweetness, but still more with circumspection.

But though you have might at your disposal, says the Sage, *you judge with clemency, and with much lenience you govern us.* [32] You are endowed with an infinite strength that nothing can resist but with us you do not use the absolute power of your sovereign authority. You treat us with extreme condescension and adapting yourself to the weakness of nature, design to place each one of us in the best and most suitable situation for working out our salvation. You dispose of us with great favor as persons who at your living image and of noble origin and who, because of their condition, are not to be ordered in the voice of a master as if they were slaves, but with care and consideration. You treat us with the same circumspection as one handles a vase of precious crystal or fragile pottery for fear of breaking it. When it is necessary for our good for you to afflict us or send us some illness or make us suffer some loss or pain, you always do so with a certain respect and a kind of deference. As a surgeon who has to operate on a person of importance takes extra care to cause him as little suffering as possible and only what is strictly necessary for his recovery, or as a father unwillingly punishes a son he loves dearly only because he is obliged to do so for his son's good, so God treats us as noble beings for whom He has the highest regard, or as beloved children *whom he chastises because he loves them.* [33]

Trials *and* Punishments Are Blessings *from* God And Proof *of* His Mercy

Looking, St. Paul tells us, *towards the author and finisher of faith, Jesus* (the only begotten and beloved Son in whom the Father is well pleased) *Consider then him who endured such opposition from sinners against himself, so that you may not grow weary and lose heart. For you have not yet resisted unto blood* (as He did) *in the struggle with sin, and you have forgotten the exhortation that is addressed to you as sons, saying, My son, neglect not the discipline of the Lord, neither be thou weary when thou art rebuked by him.*

---

[30] *Ps. 110:2*
[31] *Wis. 8:1*
[32] *Wis. 12:18*
[33] *Apoc. 3:19*

For whom the Lord loves he chastises, and he scourges every son whom he receives. Continue under discipline, for God deals with you as with sons; for what son is there whom his father does not correct?[34] In short, the purpose for which God acts is a high and holy one, His own glory and the good of His creatures. Infinitely good – Goodness itself – He seeks to make them all perfect by drawing them towards Him and making them sharers in His divinity as far as they are capable. But because of the close ties He has established with us by the union of our nature with His in the person of his Son, we in a still more special manner are the object of His benevolence and tender care. A glove is not more fitted to a hand or a sword to a scabbard than what He does and ordains in us and for us is suited to our strength and capabilities, so that everything may serve to our advantage and perfection if we but cooperate with the designs of his providence.

Our Trials Are Never Greater Than
Our Strength *to* Bear Them

Do not let ourselves be troubled when we are sometimes beset by adversity, for we know that it is meant for our spiritual welfare and carefully proportioned to our needs, and that a limit has been set to it by the wisdom of the same God who has set a bound to the ocean. Sometimes it might seem as if the sea in its fury would overflow and flood the land, but it respects the limits of its shore and its waves break upon the yielding sand. There is no tribulation or temptation whose limits God has not appointed so as to serve not for our destruction but for our salvation. *God is faithful* says the Apostle, *and will not permit you to be tempted* (or afflicted) *beyond your strength,*[35] but it is necessary for you to be so, since *through many tribulations we must enter the kingdom of God*[36] *in the steps of our Redeemer who said of Himself, Did not the Christ have to suffer all these things before entering into his glory?*[37] *If you refused to accept these tribulations you would be acting against your best interests. You are like a block of marble in the hands of the sculptor. The sculptor must chip, hew and smooth it to make it into a statue that is a work of art. God wishes to make us the living image of Himself. All we need to think of is to keep still in His hands while He works on us, and we can rest assured that the chisel will never strike the slightest blow that is not needed for His purposes and our sanctification; for, as St. Paul says, the will of God is your sanctification.*[38]

---

[34] *Heb. 12:2-7*
[35] *1 Cor. 10:13*
[36] *Acts. 14:21*

[37] *Luke 24:26*
[38] *1 Thes. 4:3*

II

The Great Advantages *to* Be Gained From
Entire Conformity *to* The Divine Will

1. *Man sanctifies himself by this conformity*
2. *Conformity to God's will makes us happy in this life as well*

Our sanctification is God's aim in all His dealings with us. What would He not do for His own honor and our good if we would only let Him! The heavens make no resistance to the spirits that guide them and their motion is magnificent, orderly and useful; they declare aloud the glory of God and preserve order in the universe by their influence and the invariable succession of day and night. If they resisted this guidance and instead of following the motion set for them they followed a different one, they would soon fall into the utmost confusion and destroy the world. It is the same when the will of man lets itself be guided by God's will. Then all that is in this microcosm, this "little world," all the faculties of the soul and members of the body are in the most perfect harmony and regular motion. But man quickly loses all these advantages and falls into the utmost confusion once he opposes his will to God's and turns aside from it.

1. Man Sanctifies Himself *by* This Conformity

In what does the sanctification of man and his perfection consist? "Some" says St. Francis of Sales "place it in austerity, others in giving to charity, others in frequenting the sacraments, others in prayer. But for my part I know no other perfection than loving God with all one's heart. Without this love all the virtues are only a heap of stones." The truth of this cannot be doubted. The Scriptures are full of it. *Thou shalt love the Lord thy God with thy whole heart, thy whole soul and thy whole mind. This is the greatest and the first commandment* Our Lord tells us.[39] And St. Paul: *Above all these things have charity, which is the bond of perfection.*[40]

In the same way that virtue is ennobled and perfected by the love of God, "so likewise" says Rodriguez following St. Chrysostom, "the highest, purest and most excellent part of this love is absolute conformity to the divine will and having in all things no other will but God's." For, as theologians teach with Pseudo-Dionysius and St. Jerome, "the chief

---

[39] *Matt. 22~37-38*   [40] *Col. 314*

effect of love is to unite the hearts of those who love each other so that they have the same will." Hence the more we submit to God's designs for us, the more we advance towards perfection. When we resist we go backward.

"Whoever makes a habit of prayer" says the great St. Teresa of Avila, "should think only of doing everything to conform his will to God's. Be assured that in this conformity consists the highest perfection we can attain, and those who practice it with the greatest care will be favored by God's greatest gift and will make the quickest progress in the interior life. Do not imagine there are other secrets. All our good consists in this."

It is related of Blessed Stephanie of Soncino, a Dominican nun, that she was one day carried in spirit to Heaven to see the happiness of the saints. She saw their souls mingling with the choirs of angels according to each one's degree of merit, and noticed among the Seraphim several persons she had known before their deaths. Having asked why these souls were raised to such a high degree of glory, she was told it was because of the conformity and perfect union of their will with God's while they lived on earth. Now, if this conformity to the will of God raises souls to the highest degree of glory in heaven among the Seraphim, it must be concluded that it raises them on earth to the highest degree of grace and on it is founded the highest perfection man can attain.

Since it is the most perfect act of charity and the most pleasing and acceptable sacrifice that is given to man to offer to God, there can be no doubt that whoever practices entire submission to His will lays up inestimable treasures at every moment and amasses more riches in a few days than others are able to acquire in many years and with great labor. To remain indifferent to good fortune or to adversity by accepting it all from the hand of God without questioning, not to ask for things to be done as we would like them but as God wishes, to make the intention of all our prayers that God's will should be perfectly accomplished in ourselves and in all creatures is to find the secret of happiness and content. *He fulfills the desire of those who fear him* says the Psalmist, *He hears their cry and saves them. The Lord keeps all who love him.*[41] And again: *We know that for those who love God all things work together unto good.*[42]

---

[41] *Ps. 144:19-20*   [42] *Rom. 8:28*

2. Conformity *to* God's Will Makes Us Happy *in* This Life *as* Well

The conforming of our will to God's is not limited to the attainment of our eternal salvation. It also has the effect of making us happy on this earth. It will give us the most perfect peace it is possible to experience in life and is the means of making this world a foretaste of heaven.

O that thou hadst hearkened to my commandments! God said to Israel, *Thy peace had been as a river.* [43] Eliphaz, one of Job's three friends, likewise says to him: *Come to terms with him to be at peace... for then you shall delight in the Almighty and you shall lift up your face towards God.* [44] It is this that the angels sang at the birth of our Savior: *Glory to God in the highest and on earth peace to men of good will.* [45] Who are these men of good will but those whose wills are in harmony with the supremely good will of God? A will that is otherwise disposed must necessarily be a bad will, incapable of obtaining the peace promised to men of *good will.*

In order for us to enjoy peace and calm we need to have nothing opposing our will and everything done in the way we want it. But who can expect to have such happiness except the man whose will is entirely conformed to the will of God? *Remember the former age for I am God and there is no God besides.... Who show from the beginning the things that shall be at last, and from ancient times the things that as yet are not done, saying: My counsel shall stand, and all my will shall be done.* [46] Every will that tries to oppose the will of God is bound to be overcome and broken, and instead of peace and happiness its effort can only end in humiliation and bitterness. *God is wise in heart and mighty in strength. Who has withstood him and remained unscathed?* [47] He, and he alone, whose will is perfectly united to God's *possesses the peace of God which surpasses all understanding.* [48] He alone can say with God Himself *all my will shall be done,* because wishing all that God wishes and only what God wishes, his wishes are always fulfilled and nothing can happen that he does not wish.

No harm befalls the just, [49] or disturbs the serenity of his mind, for if he has exactly what he wishes, he cannot be unhappy in spite of himself. It is obvious that unhappiness comes not from what others feel but from what we feel ourselves. Whatever our situation is, we must be happy if we are just as we wish to be. Certainly, we will still feel pain and sorrow, but they affect us only in the lower part of our being without being able

---

[43] *Is. 48:18*
[44] *Job 22:21-26*
[45] *Luke 2:14*
[46] *Is. 46:9-10*

[47] *Job 9:4*
[48] *Phil. 4:7*
[49] *Prov. 12:21*

to influence the mind. Obedient and resigned to the will of His Father, our Savior did not cease to be filled with the utmost joy and happiness in the midst of the most grievous sufferings it is possible to imagine.

It cannot be denied however that human nature finds the idea of suffering, humiliation, even poverty, almost incompatible with the idea of happiness, so that it is really a miracle of grace when we can be happy in such circumstances. But this miracle always mercifully accompanies the sacrifices of one who seeks to do the will of God in all things, for it is to God's honor and glory that those who give themselves generously to His service should be content with their lot.

It may perhaps be asked how it is possible to reconcile this with the words of Christ: *If anyone wishes to come after me, let him deny himself and take up his cross daily and follow me.*[50] If in this place our divine Master requires His disciples to deny themselves and carry His cross after Him, elsewhere He promises solemnly to give them not only *life everlasting* but a *hundredfold* all things they deny themselves to please Him in this life.[51] He further promises to ease the burden of His cross so as to lighten it; for He not only says that *His yoke is sweet* but adds that *His burden is light.*[52] If then we do not experience the sweetness of Christ's yoke nor the lightness of the burden of the cross, it must be because we have not yet made the denial of our will and completely given up our human outlook so as to consider things in the light of faith.

This divine light would enable us to *give thanks to God in all things*[53] as we are taught by St. Paul, He requires of us. It would be for us the beginning of that great *joy* that the Apostle urges us to have always.[54]

---

[50] *Luke 9:23*
[51] *Matt. 19:29*
[52] *id. 11:30*

[53] *1 Thes. 5:18*
[54] *id. 5:16*

III

The Practice *of* Conformity *to* The Will *of* God

1. *In the natural incidents in our daily lives*
2. *In public calamities*
3. *In the cares and difficulties of family life*
4. *In reverses of fortune*
5. *In poverty and its hardships*
6. *In adversity and disgrace*
7. *In defects of nature*
8. *In sickness and infirmity*
9. *In death and the manner of it*
10. *In the loss of spiritual consolation*
11. *In the consequences of our sins*
12. *In interior trials*
13. *In spiritual favors*
14. *Summary and conclusion*

To the question, "In what things should we practice conformity to the will of God?" there can be only one answer: "In everything."

The first thing that God asks of us is that we should faithfully keep his commandments and those of the Church, humbly obey those who have authority over us, and carefully fulfill the duties of our state.

Thereafter we should desire what God does and accept with filial submission all that is decided by His Providence. Let us now see some of the circumstances which may arise.

1. In *the* Natural Incidents *of* Our Daily Lives

In a spirit of conformity to His holy will we should accustom ourselves for the love of God to putting up with all the little daily vexations, such as a word said that wounds our self-esteem, a fly that annoys us, the barking of a dog, knocking into something as we walk along, a small accidental hurt, a light suddenly going out, a rent in our clothes, a pen that won't write, and so on. In one way it is even more important to practice conformity to God's will in these small things than in larger ones, both because they are more frequent and because the habit of supporting them in a Christian spirit prepares us in advance and in a natural manner to show resignation when we have to face serious difficulties.

We should wish with the divine will for heat and cold, storm and calm, and all the vagaries and inclemencies of the elements. We should in short accept whatever kind of weather God sends us, instead of supporting it with impatience or anger as we usually do when it is contrary to what we desire. We should avoid saying, for instance, "What awful heat!" "What terrible cold!" "What shocking weather!" "Just my bad luck!" and other expressions of the same kind which only serve to show our lack of faith and of submission to God's will.

Not only should we wish the weather to be as it is because God has made it so but, whatever inconvenience it may cause us, we should repeat with the three youths in the fiery furnace: *Cold, heat, snow and ice, lightnings and clouds, winds and tempests, bless the Lord; praise and exalt him above all forever.* [55] The elements themselves are blessing and glorifying God by doing His holy will, and we also should bless and glorify Him in the same way. Besides, even if the weather is inconvenient for us, it may be convenient for someone else. If it prevents us from doing what we want to do, it may be helping another. And even if it were not so, it should be enough for us that it is giving glory to God and that it is God who wishes it to be as it is.

St. Francis Borgia, the third General of the Society of Jesus, provides us a good example in this matter. He was once traveling to a house of the Society when it was snowing hard and bitterly cold, and his arrival was delayed until a late hour of the night when everybody was in bed and asleep. He had to wait some time before his knocking aroused someone to let him in, and then to the apologies for keeping him waiting so long in such foul weather he answered cheerfully that it was a great consolation to him to think that it was God who had dropped so much snow on him.

This practice of conformity to His will is so pleasing to God that it often has a visible influence on the material things of life. There is a story in the Lives of the Desert Fathers of a laborer whose fields always gave better crops than those of his neighbors. When asked the reason he replied that he always had whatever kind of season or weather he chose. "I never wish for any other kind of weather but what God wishes" he explained, "and as I wish for everything that pleases God, He too gives me the sort of crop that pleases me."

---

[55] *Dan. 3:67 et seq.*

2. In Public Calamities

We ought to conform to God's will in all public calamities such as war, famine and pestilence, and reverence and adore His judgments with deep humility in the firm belief that, however severe they may seem, the God of infinite goodness would not send such disasters unless some great good were to result from them. Consider how many souls may be saved through tribulation which would otherwise be lost, how many persons through affliction are converted to God and die with sincere repentance for their sins. What may appear a scourge and punishment is often a sign of great grace and mercy.

As far as we are personally concerned, let us meditate well on this truth of our faith that *the very hairs of our head are numbered,*[56] and not one of them will fall except by the will of God. In other words, we cannot suffer the least harm unless He wills and orders it. Relying on this truth we can easily understand that we have nothing more or less to fear in times of public calamity than at any other time. God can just as easily protect us in the midst of general ruin and despair as He can deliver us from evil while all around is peace and content. The only thing we need to be concerned about is to gain His favor, and this is the inevitable effect of conforming our will to His. Let us therefore hasten to accept from His hand all that He sends us, and as a result of our trustful surrender He will either cause us to gain the greatest advantages from our misfortunes or else spare us them altogether.

3. In *the* Cares *and* Difficulties *of* Family Life

If you are the father or mother of a family, you ought to conform your will to God's with regard to the number or sex of the children He pleases to give you. When men were animated by the spirit of faith they regarded a large family as a gift of God and a blessing from heaven, and considered God more than themselves as the father of their children. But now that faith has weakened and people live isolated from God, or if they think of Him at all it is mostly to fear Him and hardly ever to have trust in His providence, they are reduced to bearing the burden of their families alone. And as a man's resources, however ample and assured they may seem, are always limited and uncertain, even those who are most favored by fortune view with dismay an increase in their family. They regard it as a kind of disaster which fills them with apprehension, an

---

[56] *Matt. 10:30*

endless source of worry to poison their existence. How different it would be if we realized God's paternal treatment of those who submit to Him with filial trust! If we did so we should realize also what St. Paul meant when he said that *God is able to make all grace abound in you, so that always having ample means, you may abound in every good work.* [57]

To obtain the help of Providence it should be your aim to cooperate, as it were, with the Fatherhood of God and bring up your children as He would wish them brought up, especially by showing them good example. Have the courage to lay aside all other ambition and let this be the only object of your care and desire. Then, whatever the number of your children, you can rest assured that their heavenly Father will provide for them. He will watch over them and dispose all things for their happiness and welfare, and the more unreservedly you entrust their future to His hands, the greater will be His loving care for them.

Avoid worrying, then, about anything else for your children except whatever may contribute to bringing them up virtuously. For the rest... having entrusted them to God try to see what His will for them is, to help them along the path in life He has chosen for them. Never be afraid of relying too much on Him, but rather seek always to increase your trust more and more, for this is the most pleasing homage you can pay Him and it will be the measure of the graces you will receive. Little or much will be given you according as you have expected little or much.

4. In Reverses *of* Fortune

We should accept with the same conformity to the will of God the loss of employment or money and all other set-backs in our temporal affairs, repeating with faith the words of Job: *The Lord has given and the Lord has taken away; as it has pleased the Lord, so is it done. Blessed be the name of the Lord!* What does it matter why those who are the instruments of your reverse of fortune have acted as they have done? The revolt of Absalom and the curses of Semei were directed against David for a political purpose but this did not prevent him from attributing them, rightly, to the will of God. The misfortunes of Job were brought about by the devil because he was a just and God-fearing man. In the times of persecution Christians were deprived of rank and position, despoiled of their possessions, torn from their families, thrown into prison and sent to execution all for their religious convictions and faith in Christ. Far from

---

[57] *2 Cor. 9:8*

complaining, *they went their way*, like the apostles, *rejoicing that they had been counted worthy to suffer disgrace for the name of Jesus.* [58] Whatever the excuse for the persecution you may be made to suffer, and especially if it is because of your religion, accept it all without hesitation as coming from the understanding and paternal hand of your Father who is in heaven.

It is the same with regard to money matters. You may find yourself obliged to make a payment you consider unjust – something you have already paid but cannot prove, the forfeit of a security you have given for someone, or taxes you consider excessive, or anything of this nature. If the payment can be, and is, lawfully required of you, then it is the will of God you should pay it. It is He who is asking you for the money and it is to Him you are really giving it when you bow to the necessity in a spirit of submission to His will. Those who act in this way can be assured of His manifold graces. Let us take the case of two persons. One, out of a spirit of conformity perhaps excessive, perhaps quite unfair, but which his creditor has the power to demand. The other, of his own free choice, gives an equal sum to charity. It is well known what great advantages, even in this life, are to be gained from giving to charity, but the person who makes a sacrifice of his money not of his own accord or to someone he chooses to give it, but out of a spirit of conformity to God's will, is performing an even more profitable act. By the very fact that it is against his will, the act is purer and more agreeable in the sight of God, and if it can be said that from the experiences of all ages charity brings down upon man the abundant blessing of God, it can also be said without exaggeration that such an act as has been described brings down still more abundant blessings.

5. In Poverty *and* Its Hardships

We ought to conform to God's will in poverty and all the inconveniences poverty brings in its train. It is not too hard to do so if we fully realize that God watches over us as a father over his children and puts us in that condition because it is of most value to us. Poverty then takes on a different aspect in our eyes, for by looking on the privations it imposes as salutary remedies we even cease to think of ourselves as poor.

If a rich man has a son in bad health and prescribes a strict diet for him, does the son think he has to eat small amounts of plain or tasteless food because his father cannot afford better? Does he begin to worry about how he will exist in the future? Will other people think that

---

[58] *Acts 5:41*

22

because of his diet he has become poor? Everybody knows how well off his father is and that he shares in his father's wealth and he will again have what is now forbidden him as soon as his health is restored.

Are we not the children of the God of riches, the co-heirs of Christ? Being so, is there anything we can lack? Let it be said boldly: whoever responds to his divine adoption with the feelings of love and trust that the position of being children of God demands has a right, here and now, to all that God Himself possesses. Everything then is ours. But it is not expedient we should enjoy everything. It is often necessary we should be deprived of many things. Let us be careful not to conclude from the privations imposed on us only as remedies that we may ever be in want of anything that is to our advantage. Let us firmly believe that if anything is necessary or really useful for us, our all-powerful Father will give it to us without fail. To those gathered round to hear Him our Savior said: *If you evil as you are, know how to give good gifts to your children, how much more will your heavenly Father...?*[59]

This is an unquestionable truth of our holy faith, and any doubt about it, through lack of confidence on our part, can only be blameworthy and an insult to Christ who again and again made the most definite promises about the matter. *Do not be anxious for your life, what you shall eat* He tells us, *nor yet for your body, what you shall put on. Look at the birds of the air; they do not sow or reap or gather into barns, yet your heavenly Father feeds them. Are not you of much more value than they?... And as for clothing, why are you anxious? Consider how the lilies of the field grow; they neither toil nor spin, yet I say to you that not even Solomon in all his glory was arrayed like one of these. But if God so clothes the grass of the field, which flourishes today but tomorrow is thrown into the oven, how much more you, O you of little faith! Therefore do not be anxious, saying, 'What shall we eat?' or 'What shall we drink? or 'What are we to put on?', for after all these things the Gentiles seek; but your Father knows that you need all these things.*[60] He has given His word and there is only one condition attached – that we *seek first the kingdom of God and his justice,* that we make this search the one great aim of our lives by bringing everything else into relation with it to make it successful and fulfil our every duty with this end in view. In return for this He will unburden us of all anxiety, He will take upon Himself all our needs and the needs of those who belong to us or for whom we have to provide, and His care will be all the greater in

[59] Luke 11:13   [60] Matt 6:25-32; Luke 12:22-30

proportion to the degree of confidence and surrender to His will we strive to attain.

Do we then for love of Him give up the desire to possess the perishable goods of this world? By virtue of another of Christ's promises these goods *a hundredfold,* as well as *eternal life,* are assured us in this life, and as a result we shall be rich while we are judged to be poor. Freed from the thirst for wealth, from the possession of it and the burden that accompanies it, we shall enjoy a peace and contentment unknown to those who, appearing to possess riches, are in reality possessed by them and cannot escape the cares they bring with them. In this way we shall experience the truth of St. Paul's words that *godliness has the promise of the present life as well as of that which is to come.*[61]

6. In Adversity *and* Disgrace

We ought to conform to the will of God in adversity as well as in prosperity, in humiliation as well as in honor, in disgrace as well as in respect. We should willingly accept all things as being the ordering of Providence, so as to give God by our submission the honor due to Him, and at the same time attain without fail our greatest good.

When David left Jerusalem to escape the attack of his son Absalom, the Ark of the Covenant was carried after him by the order of Sadoc the High Priest so that it might serve as a safeguard for the king in his imminent danger and be a pledge of his safe return. But David told Sadoc to take the ark back, because God would see to his return if He so wished, and then he added: *But if the Lord shall say to me: 'Thou pleasest me not' —* I have withdrawn my favor from you, I will not have you reign longer over my people, I will take away your power and give it to your enemy — *I am ready. Let him do that which is good before him.'*[62] We should say the same in whatever circumstances we find ourselves, and above all take care not to refuse on the specious pretext that we are not capable of such heroic resignation. God Himself will accomplish it in us provided we do not oppose resistance to His grace.

This is the point of the story that Cassian tells us about the old man who was attacked by a mob of pagans in Alexandria. He remained calm and unruffled in spite of insults and blows. Someone asked him mockingly what miracles Christ had worked. "He has just worked one" the old man replied, "for in spite of all you have done to me, I haven't been angry with you or the least bit upset."

[61] *1 Tim. 4:8*   [62] *2 Kings 15:26*

7. In Defects *of* Nature

Our conformity to the will of God should extend to our natural defects, mental ones included. We should not, for example, complain or feel grieved at not being so clever or so witty or not having such a good memory as other people. Why should we complain of the little that has fallen to our lot when we have deserved nothing of what God has given us? Is not all a free gift of His generosity for which we are greatly indebted to Him? What services has He received from us that He should have made us a human being rather than some lower animal? Have we done anything to oblige Him to give us existence itself?

But it is not enough just not to complain. We ought to be content with what we have been given and desire nothing more. What we have is sufficient because God has judged it so. Just as a workman uses the shape and size of tool best suited to the job in hand, so God gives us those qualities which are in accordance with the designs He has for us. The important thing is to use well what He has given us. It may be added that it is very fortunate for some people to have only mediocre qualities or limited talents. The measure of them that God has given will save them, while they might be ruined if they had more. Superiority of talent very often only serves to engender pride and vanity and so become a means of perdition.

8. Sickness *and* Infirmity

We ought to conform to the will of God in sickness and infirmity and wish for what He sends us, both at the time it comes and for the time it lasts and with all the circumstances attending it, without wishing for one of them to be changed; and at the same time do all that is reasonable in our power to get well again, because God wishes it so. "For my part" says St. Alphonsus, "I call illness the touchstone of the spirit, for it is then that the true virtue of a man is discovered." If we feel ourselves becoming impatient or rebellious, we should endeavor to repress such feelings and be deeply ashamed of any attempt at opposition to the just decrees of an all-wise God.

St. Bonaventure relates that St. Francis of Assisi was afflicted by an illness which caused him great pain. One of his followers said to him, "Ask Our Lord to treat you a little more gently, for it seems to me He lays His hand too heavily upon you." Hearing this the saint gave a cry and addressed the man in these words: "If I did not think that what you have just said comes from the simplicity of your heart without any evil

25

intention, I would have no more to do with you, because you have been so rash as to find fault with what God does to me." Then, though he was very weak from the length and violence of his illness, he threw himself down from the rough bed he was lying on, at the risk of breaking his bones, and kissing the floor of his cell said "I thank you, O Lord, for all the sufferings you send me. I beg you to send me a hundred times more if you think it right. I shall rejoice if it pleases you to afflict me without sparing me in any way, for the accomplishment of your holy will is my greatest consolation."

And in fact if, as St. Ephraim observes, a mule-driver knows how much his mule can carry and does not try to kill it by overloading it, and if the potter knows how long the clay should bake to be suitable for use and does not leave it longer in the kiln than is necessary, then it would show very little appreciation of God to venture to think that He who is wisdom itself and loves us with an infinite love would load our backs with too heavy a burden or leave us longer than is necessary in the fire of tribulation. We can be quite sure that the fire will not last longer or be hotter than is necessary to bake our clay to the right point.

9. In Death *and* The Manner *of* It

We ought to carry our conformity to God's will to the point of accepting our death. That we shall die is a decree against which there is no appeal. We shall die on the day and at the hour and in the manner that God decides, and it is this particular death we should accept, because it is the one most becoming His glory. One day when St. Gertrude was climbing a hill she slipped and fell down to the bottom. She was unhurt and began to climb up again saying: "What great happiness it would have been for me, O Lord, if this fall had been the means of bringing me sooner to thee!" Her companions asked her if she was not afraid of dying without receiving the last sacraments. "I would certainly wish with all my heart to receive them in my last moments," she answered, "but I much prefer the will of God, for I am sure the best disposition for a good death is submission to His will. So, I desire only the death by which He wishes me to come to Him, and I am confident that in whatever way I die, His mercy will not fail me."

Even more, it is the teaching of great masters of the spiritual life that a person who, at the point of death, makes an act of perfect conformity to the will of God will be delivered not only from hell but also from purgatory, even if he has committed all the sins in the world. "The reason," says St. Alphonsus, "is that he who accepts death with perfect resignation acquires similar merit to that of a martyr who has voluntarily given his life for Christ, and even amid the greatest sufferings he will die happily and joyfully."

10. In *the* Loss *of* Spiritual Consolation

We ought to practice conformity to the will of God when we are deprived of those exterior aids to our spiritual well-being that He pleases to withdraw from us. For example, a friend or counsellor on whom you rely for help and encouragement is taken away from you and you seem unable to get along without him. There is, in fact, some truth in what you feel, in that you really need the help of someone, and the friend or counsellor had been given to you for that very reason. But does God love you less now than He did when He made the gift? Is He no longer your Father? Or does such a Father as He is desert His children? Your guide and friend has been of value to you so far, but is he the right person to help you in what you are called to do now? Christ our divine Master said of Himself to His apostles *It is expedient for you that I depart, for if I do not go, the Advocate will not come to you, but if I go I will send him to you.*[63] Who then can venture to say that it is not an advantage for him to lose a friend or spiritual adviser, however excellent, wise or holy he may be?

But, you may answer, how do I know it is not a punishment my sins have brought on me? It may well be so, but the punishments of a father become salutary remedies for obedient children. If you wish to stay the anger of your heavenly Father, soften His heart and even oblige Him to send you fresh graces, then accept your punishment, and in return for your trustful surrender to Him He will either find you someone to help you even better than before, or He Himself in His goodness will deign to be your guide. He will send you His Holy Spirit as He sent Him to His apostles. He will enlighten your path and fortify you by the action of His grace.

Let us take another example. You are living a good Christian life in the practice of your religion. You fall seriously ill and cannot frequent the Sacraments or assist at Mass — perhaps you feel too weak even to pray. But do not grieve. You are called to the honor of nourishing your soul by partaking, with Christ Himself, of *a food that*, perhaps, *you know not of*, and which will be the means of making your illness a powerful

---

[63] *John 16:7*

means of sanctification. *My food* He said to His disciples, *is to do the will of Him who sent me.* [64] It is the same food that is offered to you, and note well that it is only by this food that it is given to us to live to eternal life. Prayer itself is valueless unless it is vitalized by this health-giving food, as our Savior explained when He said: *Not everyone who says to me 'Lord, Lord' shall enter into the kingdom of heaven, but he who does the will of my Father in heaven shall enter the kingdom of heaven.* [65] If then it is God who has placed you in the condition you are in, it is He who dispenses you from the practices of your religion, nay, forbids them. So you should not worry, but remember that in exchange He expects you to take more care in doing His will by giving up your own.

It is in order that you may make the doing of His will your chief food that the means to do it are so frequently given. How many inconveniences and sacrifices are in fact imposed upon us by illness! – plans upset, expense incurred, unpleasant remedies, perhaps, loneliness and lack of care – a host of large and small annoyances. There are so many opportunities to say, 'God wishes it so. His will be done.' Do not let any of these opportunities pass and you will be among those souls most dear to Christ. *For whoever* He said, *does the will of my Father who is in heaven, he is my brother, my sister, and my mother.* [66]

Let us take another example. Some great feast-day or solemnity is approaching and you prepare yourself in anticipation of the joyful event. But when the day arrives you no longer feel the same as you did before. Your fervor has given place to disinterest and spiritual dryness and you are incapable of a single good thought. Do not try to force yourself out of this state. It has been produced in you by God, and we know that all that comes from Him is good, so it must be to your advantage if you submit to it.

Accept the situation from His hand, endeavoring as far as possible to be recollected in His presence and submitting yourself to Him as a patient who awaits the healing action of the doctor, and you can rest assured that no spiritual consolation will ever be so profitable to you as the dryness cheerfully born in a spirit of conformity to His will. It is not what we feel that prepares us for God's grace, but the act of our will, and this act is not one of feeling. It may well be accompanied by pleasurable sentiments, but this adds nothing to the merit of it. In the sight of God, the absence

[64] *id. 4:32,34*
[65] *Matt. 7:21*

[66] *id. 12:50*

28

of this sentiment or even the presence of contrary ones which we do not wish to have in no way minimizes the value of the act itself.

Let us realize this fact, that prayer has no need of feeling in order to be of value. It consists solely in the movement of the will towards God, and by its nature this movement has nothing to do with feeling. God's grace operates in us in the same way. It may be compared to the effects produced in us by the food we eat. We do not feel the food inside our bodies while it is engaged in its hidden work of restoring and fortifying; and in the same way Christ, our heavenly food, who is given to us for our spiritual nourishment, works hiddenly in our souls. But the trouble is we want to feel everything, and when we experience no feeling of satisfaction, we either get discouraged or try by long and forced prayers to produce something inside ourselves to reassure us. Such efforts impede rather than aid the operation of grace by occupying and agitating our minds too much.

It is related of St. Catherine of Siena that one day she asked Our Lord why it was that God had so often revealed Himself to the patriarchs, prophets and Christians of early times but rarely did so in her own time. Our Lord replied that it was because they were devoid of self-esteem and came to Him as faithful disciples to await His inspiration, allowing themselves to be fashioned like gold in the crucible or painted on by His hands like an artist's canvas, and letting Him write the law of love in their hearts.

But the Christians of her time acted as if He could not see or hear them, and wanted to do and say everything by themselves, keeping themselves so busy and restless that they would not allow Him to work in them. Note that Our Savior had already tried to warn us against such excess in the Gospel when He said *When you pray, do not multiply words as the Gentiles do; for they think that by saying a great deal they will be heard. So do not be like them for your Father knows what you need before you ask Him.*[67]

11. In *the* Consequences *of* Our Sins

With submission and conformity to the will of God we should bear the evil consequences of which falling into sin is often the cause. It may be some indisposition or some more serious effect on our health brought about by over-indulgence; some sacrifice we have to make because of

---

[67] *id.* 6:7

29

money spent foolishly for selfish ends; some bad turn in our affairs owing to impatient or imprudent conduct on our part; difficulty in resisting temptation and leading a good life because of a long habit of sin we have contracted – the situation fills us with worry and anxiety and we feel unable to cope with it. God certainly did not wish you should sin, but the sin having been committed, He wishes for your good that it should be followed by this punishment. Accept it then from His hand in the belief that there is nothing more suited to regaining His favor than your humble acceptance of it. Then, far from being prejudicial to you, your failures, in so far as they give you the opportunity of submitting to His will, will be as it were a monument to your perseverance in God's service, and the more numerous they have been, the more glorious will be their witness to your perseverance.

Let us take a practical example. A man has to make a journey on foot. He must go across rough country, he is without food and almost exhausted, so he falls repeatedly. But he gets to his feet again each time, determined not to give in and, come what may, arrive at his destination. When he finally arrives, is it not true to say that his perseverance has been all the greater and more heroic in proportion to the number of obstacles he has had to overcome and the falls from which he has recovered?

12. In Interior Trials

We ought to conform to God's will in interior trials, that is to say in all the difficulties met with in our spiritual life, such as temptations, scruples, anxieties, aridity, desolation and so on. Whatever immediate cause we may attribute to these states of mind, we must always look beyond to God as their author. If we think they come from ourselves, then it is true to say that they have their origin in the ignorance of our mind, the over-sensitiveness of our feelings, the disordered state of our imagination or the perversity of our inclinations. But if we go back farther, if we ask where the defects themselves come from, we can only find their origin in the will of God who has not endowed us with greater perfection, and by making us subject to these infirmities has laid on us the duty of bearing all the consequences of them for our sanctification until He is pleased to put an end to them. As soon as He judges it the right moment to touch our mind or heart, we shall be enlightened, fortified and consoled.

Even if we suppose that our disturbed state is the work of the devil, it must still be attributed to God. Does not the history of Job show that Satan has no power over us unless God gives it to him? When Saul was beset by temptations of jealousy and hate towards David, the Scriptures tell us, *the evil spirit from God came upon Saul.*[68] But if the spirit was from God, how could it be evil? And if it was evil, how could it be from God? It is evil because of the devil's evil and depraved will to afflict men in order to bring them to perdition, and it is from God because God allows him to afflict them in His plan of salvation for them.

Moreover, we learn from the principles of our faith and the teaching of the saints that often God Himself by His immediate action withdraws the visible effects of His grace for purposes in accordance with His wisdom and goodness. How many persons who have become lukewarm and careless in their duties are roused by the awareness of God's absence and are able to regain the fervor they had lost! How many more have been led to the practice of the highest virtue by interior trials! Who can measure the degree of heroic virtue saints like St. Ignatius, St. Teresa or St. Francis of Sales attained by this means? We must consider it the action of a Providence unceasingly attentive to the welfare of His children, who feigns to abandon them in order to rouse them from slumber or increase their humility, self-distrust and self-renouncement, their confidence in God, submission to His will and perseverance in prayer. Hence instead of allowing ourselves to become discouraged and faint-hearted under trials which may seem to overwhelm us, let us act in the same way as we do when our bodies are sick, consult a good doctor — a good spiritual director — and applying the remedies he advises, patiently await the effects that it pleases God to give.

Everything is meant for our good, and such trials ought to be counted as special graces from God. Whether or not they are sent as a punishment for our sins, they come from Him and we should thank Him for them, placing ourselves entirely in His hands. If we bear them with patience, we shall receive greater grace than if we were filled with a sense of fervent devotion.

13. In Spiritual Favors

Finally — and this is perhaps the most difficult aspect of what concerns the practice of conformity to the will of God — we should desire virtue itself and the degrees of grace only in so far as God wishes to give

---

[68] *1 Kings 18:10*

them, and not desire more. Our whole ambition should be to attain the degree of perfection that has been appointed for us, since it has not been given to everybody to reach the same height. It is obvious that however well we may correspond with the graces given us, we can never equal the humility, charity and other virtues of the Blessed Virgin. And who can even presume to imagine that he can reach the same heights as the apostles? Who can equal St. John the Baptist whom Christ called the greatest of the children of men? Or St. Joseph to whom God entrusted His Son? In this we must as in all else submit to the will of God. He must be able to say of us, *My will is in them*; it rules and governs everything.

So, when we hear or read that God in a short time has brought some souls to a very high degree of perfection and shown them signal favors, enlightened their understanding and imbued their hearts with His love, we should repress any desire to be treated likewise so as not to fall short in pure love of conformity to His will. We should even unite ourselves still more closely to His will by saying, "I praise Thee, O Lord, and bless Thee for deigning to show Thyself with so great love and familiarity to the souls Thou hast chosen. The honor you show them is above all measure, but the accomplishment of Thy holy will is of more concern to me than all the marks of favor Thou hast shown Thy saints. The only favor I ask is that in no single thing should I ever do my own will and that my will be entirely at one with Thine. Let others ask for what they wish, but my sole request is that I may wish what Thou wishest and Thy purposes may be accomplished perfectly in me. Do with me, in me, and by me all that Thou wilt without resistance from me, in time and in eternity."

14. Summary *and* Conclusion

This submission and conformity in all things to His will is so pleasing to God that it gained for David the honor of being called 'a man after His heart.' *I have found*, He says, *David the son of Jesse, a man after my heart who will do all that I desire.*[69] David, in fact, was so obedient to the commands of Providence that his heart was like wax, ever ready to receive indifferently any impression from the hand of God. *My heart is steadfast, O God, my heart is steadfast*, he exclaims.[70] St. Bernard asks why in this verse of the psalm David twice repeats the words *My heart is steadfast*, and replies that by this repetition he meant he was ready to accept bad fortune as well as good, disgrace as well as honor, and was

---

[69] *1 Kings 16:12; Acts 13:22*   [70] *Ps. 56:8; 107:2*

prepared for all that God willed. Let us, too, enter resolutely into the state of steadfastness which rejoices the heart of our heavenly Father and will be the means of our sanctification, the source of peace and joy in this world and the pledge of our eternal happiness in the next.

It is useful for this purpose to familiarize ourselves with those phrases in Scripture where conformity to the will of God is expressed in the clearest manner. We can say, for example, with St. Paul, *Lord, what wilt thou have me to do?*[71] I am ready to do whatever you will. Or with David, *I was like a brute beast in your presence*[72] not questioning, and obeying unresistingly. *I am thine; do with me according to thy good pleasure.*[73] I seek *not my own will,* said Our Savior, *I have come down from heaven not to do my own will but the will of Him who sent me. My food is to do the will of my Father who is in heaven.*[74] Following our divine model let us make our food the accomplishment of God's will. *Father, let it be so, for such is thy good pleasure – Thy will be done on earth as it is in heaven.*[75] Our Savior recommended St. Catherine of Genoa to pause particularly on these words when she recited the Our Father. We should do the same and often pray God that His holy will may be accomplished here below in ourselves and in all creatures with the same perfection and for the same reasons that the saints accomplish it in heaven.

When we find some difficulty in obeying God or feel inclined to rebel, let us say with David, *Why art thou downcast, o my soul?* He has given you everything you have, He has provided everything for your salvation. I will not resist Him, I will obey His orders, for *He is my savior and my God;* and if human nature refuses to do what He orders, *He is my strength to overcome it.*[76] Let us say with Our Lord during His agony, *Father, not my will but thine be done*[77] "These words of our Divine Master," says the great St. Leo, "are the salvation of His whole Mystical Body, the Church. These words have instructed all the faithful, inspired all the confessors, crowned all the martyrs. Let all the Church's children, redeemed at so high a price, justified without any deserving on their part, learn these words and using them as a safe defense when they are assailed by any strong temptation, they will resist the attacks of nature and suffer tribulation with courage. In this spirit of conformity to His will we should accept not only all the incidents of our daily lives but all the inner struggles and difficulties such

---

[71] *Acts 9-6*

[72] *Ps. 72:22*

[73] *id. 118:94*

[74] *John 4:34; 5:30; 6:38*

[75] *Matt. 11:26; 6:10*

[76] *Ps. 42:2*

[77] *Luke 22:42*

resignation may cost us, because God wishes us to experience them for His glory and our own profit.

Let us note here, with regard to the difficulties we may find in submitting to the will of God, that even when our will is firmly decided to submit, and has in fact submitted, our mind, following its natural inclination, may still continue to reason and argue on the events that are occurring or may occur. We may say to ourselves for example: "If I were now well, or if I were to fall ill, if I were given such and such a job, if I were sent to such and such a place, if such and such a thing happened, it would be good (or bad) for me, it would help (or prevent) my plans, I could do this or that as I want to," and so on. Nature tries thus to obtain at least the satisfaction of thinking about and discussing the incidents of our lives. But we should endeavor to exterminate these remains of our corrupt nature, and just as for the love of God we have forbidden our will to use its freedom of choice, for the same reason we ought to deny our mind the freedom of discussion and judgment. Let us entrust ourselves totally and unreservedly to the direction of Divine Providence.

Part II

by St. Claude de la Columbière

IV Trustful Surrender *to* Divine Providence

1. Consoling truths
   Trust in God's wisdom
   When God sends us trials
   Loving recourse to God
   Practice of trustful surrender
2. Adversity is useful for the just and necessary for sinners
   We must trust in Providence
   Unexpected advantages from our trials
   Opportunities for acquiring merit and saving our souls
3. Recourse to prayer
   To obtain what we want
   To be delivered from evil
   We do not ask enough
   Perseverance in prayer
   Obstinate trust

1. Consoling Truths

It is one of the most firmly established and most consoling of the truths that have been revealed to us that (apart from sin) *nothing happens to us in life unless God wills it so.* Wealth and poverty alike come from Him. If we fall ill, God is the cause of our illness; if we get well, our recovery is due to God. We owe our lives entirely to Him, and when death comes to put an end to life, His will be the hand that deals the blow.

But should we attribute it to God when we are unjustly persecuted? Yes, He is the only person you can charge with the wrong you suffer. He is not the cause of the sin the person commits by ill-treating you, but He is the cause of the suffering that person inflicts on you while sinning.

God did not inspire your enemy with the will to harm you, but He gave him the power to do so. If you receive a wound, do not doubt but that it is God Himself who has wounded you. If all living creatures were to league themselves against you, unless the Creator wished it and joined with them and gave them the strength and means to carry out their purpose, they would never succeed. *You would have no power over me if it had not been given you from above,* the Savior of the world said to Pilate. We can say the same to demons and men, to the brute beasts and to whatever exists – You would not be able to disturb me or harm me as you do unless God had ordered it so. You are sent by Him, you are given the power by Him to tempt me and to make me suffer. *You would have no power over me if it had not been given you from above.*

If from time to time we meditated seriously on this truth of our faith it would be enough to stifle all complaint in whatever loss or misfortune we suffer. What I have the Lord gave me, it has been taken away by Him. It is not a lawsuit or a thief that has ruined you or a certain person that has slandered you; if your child dies it is not by accident or wrong treatment, but because God, to whom all belongs, has not wished you to keep it longer.

Trust in God's Wisdom

It is then a truth of our faith that God is responsible for all the happenings we complain of in the world and, furthermore, we cannot doubt that all the misfortunes God sends us have a very useful purpose. We cannot doubt it without imputing to God a lack of judgment in deciding what is advantageous for us.

It is usually the case that other people can see better than we can ourselves what is good for us. It would be foolish to think that we can see better than God Himself, who is not subject to any of the passions that blind us, knows the future and can foresee all events and the consequences of every action. Experience shows that even the gravest misfortunes can have good results and the greatest successes end in disaster. A rule also that God usually follows is to attain His ends by ways that are the opposite to those human prudence would normally choose.

In our ignorance of what the future holds, how can we be so bold as to question what comes about by God's permission? Surely it is reasonable to think that our complaints are groundless and that instead of complaining we ought to be thanking Providence. Joseph was sold into slavery and thrown into prison. If he had felt aggrieved at these apparent misfortunes, he would really have been feeling aggrieved at his happiness for they were the steps to the throne of Egypt. Saul loses his father's asses and has to go on a long vain hunt for them. But if he had felt annoyed at the great waste of time and energy it caused him, his annoyance could not have been more unreasonable as it was all a means of bringing him to the prophet who was to anoint him king of his people.

Let us imagine our confusion when we appear before God and understand the reasons why He sent us the crosses we accept so unwillingly. The death of a child will then be seen as its rescue from some great evil had it lived, separation from the woman you love the means of saving you from an unhappy marriage, a severe illness the reason for many years of life afterwards, loss of money the means of saving your soul from eternal loss. So, what are we worried about? God is looking after us and yet we are full of anxiety! We trust ourselves to a doctor because we suppose he knows his business. He orders an operation which involves cutting away part of our body and we accept it. We are grateful to him and pay him a large fee because we judge he would not act as he does unless the remedy were necessary, and we must rely on his skill. Yet we are unwilling to treat God in the same way! It looks as if we do not trust His wisdom and are afraid, He cannot do His job properly. We allow ourselves to be operated on by a man who may easily make a mistake – a mistake which may cost us our life – and protest when God sets to work on us.

If we could see all He sees we would unhesitatingly wish all He wishes. We would beg Him on bended knees for those afflictions we now ask Him to spare us. To all of us He addresses the words spoken to the Sons of Zebeedee: *You know not what you ask* – O blind of heart, your ignorance saddens me. Let me manage your affairs and look after your interests. I know what you need better than you do yourselves. If I paid heed to what you think you need you would have been hopelessly ruined long ago.

When God sends us trials

If you would be convinced that in all He allows and in all that happens to you God has no other end in view but your real advantage and your eternal happiness, reflect a moment on all He has done for you; you are now suffering, but remember that the author of this suffering is He who chose to spend His life suffering to save you from everlasting suffering, whose angel is always at your side guarding your body and soul by His order, who sacrifices Himself daily on the altar to expiate your sins and appease His Father's anger, who comes lovingly to you in the Holy Eucharist and whose greatest pleasure is to be united to you. We must be very ungrateful to mistrust Him after He has shown such proofs of His love and to imagine that He can intend us harm. But, you will say, this blow is a cruel one, He strikes too hard. What have you to fear from a hand that was pierced and nailed to the cross for you? – The path I have to tread is full of thorns. If there is no other to reach heaven by, do you prefer to perish forever rather than to suffer for a time? Is it not the same path He trod before you out of love for you? Is there a thorn in it that He has not reddened with His own blood? – The chalice He offers you is a bitter one. But remember that it is your Redeemer who offers it. Loving you as He does, could He bring Himself to treat you so severely if the need were not urgent, the gain not worthwhile? Can we dare to refuse the chalice He has prepared for us Himself?

Reflect well on this. It should be enough to make us accept and love whatever trials He intends we should suffer. Moreover, it is the certain means of securing our happiness in this life quite apart from the next.

Loving recourse to God

Let us now suppose that by these reflections and the help of God you have freed yourself from all worldly desires and can now say to yourself: All is vanity and nothing can satisfy my heart. The things that I so earnestly desire may not be at all the things that will bring me happiness. It is difficult for me to distinguish what is good from what is harmful because good and evil are nearly always mixed, and what was good for yesterday may be bad for today. My desires are only a source of worry and my efforts to realize them mostly end in failure. After all, the will of God is bound to prevail in the end. Nothing can be done without His command, and He cannot ordain anything that is not for my good.

After this let us suppose that you turn to God with blind trust and surrender yourself unconditionally and unreservedly to Him, entirely resolved to put aside your own hopes and fears; in short, determined to wish nothing except what He wishes and to wish all that He wishes. From this moment you will acquire perfect liberty and will never again be able to feel troubled or uneasy, and there is no power on earth capable of doing you violence or giving you a moment's unrest.

You may object that a person on whom both good and evil make the same impression is a pure fiction. It is nothing of the kind. I know people who are just as happy if they are sick or if they are well, if they are badly off or they are well off. I know some who even prefer illness and poverty to health and riches.

Moreover, it is all the more remarkable that the more we submit to God's will, the more He tries to meet our wishes. It would seem that as soon as we make it our sole aim to obey Him, He on His part does His best to try and please us. Not only does He answer our prayers but He even forestalls them by granting the very desires we have endeavored to stifle in our hearts in order to please Him, and granting them in a measure we had never imagined.

Finally, the happiness of the person whose will is entirely submitted to God's is constant, unchangeable and endless. No fear comes to disturb it for no accident can destroy it. He is like a man seated on a rock in the middle of the ocean who looks on the fury of the waves without dismay and can amuse himself watching and counting them as they roar and break at his feet. Whether the sea is calm or rough, whichever way the waves are carried by the wind is a matter of indifference to him, for the place where he is firm and unshakeable.

That is the reason for the peaceful and untroubled expression we find on the faces of those who have dedicated themselves to God.

Practice of trustful surrender

It remains to be seen how we can attain to this happy state. One sure way to lead us to it is the frequent practice of the virtue of submission. But as the opportunities for practicing it in a big way come rather seldom, we must take advantage of the small ones which occur daily, and which will soon put us in a position to face the greater trials with equanimity when the time comes. There is no one who does not experience a hundred small annoyances every day, caused either by our own carelessness or inattention, or by the inconsideration or spite of other people, or by pure accident. Our whole lives are made up of incidents of this kind, occurring ceaselessly from one minute to another and producing a host of involuntary feelings of dislike and aversion, envy, fear and impatience to trouble the serenity of our minds. We let an incautious word slip out and wish we had not said it; someone says something we find offensive; we have to wait a long time to be served when we are in a hurry; we are irritated by a child's boisterousness; a boring acquaintance buttonholes us in the street; a car splashes us with mud; the weather spoils our outing; our work is not going as well as we would wish; a tool breaks at a critical moment; we get our clothes torn or stained – these are not occasions for practicing heroic virtue but they can be a means of acquiring it if we wish. If we were careful to offer all these petty annoyances to God and accept them as being ordered by His providence, we would soon be in a position to support the greatest misfortunes that can happen to us, besides at the same time insensibly drawing close to intimate union with God.

To this exercise – so easy and yet so useful for us and pleasing to God – another may be added. Every morning as soon as you get up think of all the most disagreeable things that could happen to you during the day. Your house might be burnt down, you might lose your job or all your savings, or be run over, or sudden death might come to you or to a person you love. Accept these misfortunes should it please God to allow them; compel your will to agree to the sacrifice and give yourself no rest until you really feel prepared to wish or not to wish all that God may wish or not wish.

Finally, if some great misfortune should actually happen, instead of wasting time in complaint or self-pity, go throw yourself at once at the feet of your Savior and implore His grace to bear your trial with fortitude and patience. A man who has been badly wounded does not, if he is wise, chase after his assailant, but makes straight for a doctor who may save his life. Even if you wanted to confront the person responsible for your misfortune, it would still be to God you would have to go, for there can be no other cause of it than He.

So go to God, but go at once, go there and then. Let this be your first thought. Go and report to Him what He has done to you. Kiss the hands of God crucified for you, the hands that have struck you and caused you to suffer. Repeat over and over again to Him His own words to His Father while He was suffering: *Not my will but thine be done.* In all that Thou wishest of me, today and for always, in heaven and on earth, let Thy will be done, but let it be done on earth as it is done in heaven.

2. Adversity Is Useful *for* The Just *and* Necessary *for* Sinners

Imagine the anguish and tears of a mother who is present at a painful operation her child has to undergo. Can anyone doubt on seeing her that she consents to allow the child to suffer only because she expects it to get well and be spared further suffering by means of this violent remedy?

Reason in the same manner when adversity befalls you. You complain that you are ill-treated, insulted, slandered, robbed. Your Redeemer (the name is a tenderer one than that of father or mother), your Redeemer is a witness to all you are suffering. He who loves you and has emphatically declared that whoever touches you touches the apple of His eye, nevertheless allows you to be stricken though He could easily prevent it. Do you hesitate to believe that this passing trial is necessary for the health of your soul?

Even if the Holy Spirit had not called blessed those who suffer, if every page of Scripture did not proclaim aloud the necessity of adversity, if we did not see that suffering is the normal destiny of those who are friends of God, we should still be convinced that it is of untold advantage to us. It is enough to know that the God who chose to suffer all the most horrible tortures the rage of man can invent rather than see us condemned to the slightest pain in the next life is the same God who prepares and offers us the chalice of bitterness we must drink in this world. A God who has so suffered to prevent us from suffering would not make us suffer today to give Himself cruel and pointless pleasure.

We must have trust in Providence

When I see a Christian grief-stricken at the trials God sends him, I say to myself: Here is a man who is grieved at his own happiness. He is asking God to be delivered from something he ought to be thanking Him for. I am quite sure that nothing more advantageous could happen to him than what causes him so much grief. I have a hundred unanswerable reasons for saying so. But if I could read into the future and see the happy outcome of his present misfortune, how greatly strengthened I would be in my judgment! If we could discover the designs of Providence it is certain we would ardently long for the evils we are now so unwilling to suffer. We would rush forward to accept them with the utmost gratitude if we had a little faith and realized how much God loves us and has our interests at heart.

What profit can come to me from this illness which ties me down and obliges me to give up all the good I was doing, you may ask. What advantage can I expect from this ruin of my life which leaves me desperate and hopeless? It is true that sudden great misfortune at the moment it comes may appear to overwhelm you and not allow you the opportunity there and then of profiting by it. But wait a while and you will see that by it God is preparing you to receive the greatest marks of His favor. But for this accident you would not have perhaps become less good than you are, but you would not have become holy. Isn't it true that since you have been trying to lead a good Christian life there has been something you have been unwilling to surrender to God? Some worldly ambition, some pride in your attainments, some indulgence of the body, some blameworthy habit, some company that is the occasion of sin for you? It was only this final step that prevented you from attaining the perfect freedom of the love of God. It wasn't really very much, but you could not bring yourself to make this last sacrifice. It wasn't very much, but there is nothing harder for a Christian than to break the last tie that binds him to the world or to his own self. He knows he ought to do it, and until he does it there is something wrong with his life. But the very thought of the remedy terrifies him, for the malady has taken such a hold on him that it cannot be cured without the help of a serious and painful operation. So it was necessary to take you unawares, to cut deep into the flesh with skillful hand when you were least expecting it and remove the ulcer concealed within, or otherwise you would never be well. The misfortune which has befallen you will soon do what all your exercises of piety would never have been able to do.

Unexpected advantages from our trials

If the consequence of your adversity is that which was intended by God, if it turns you aside completely from creatures to give yourself unreservedly to your Creator, I am sure that your thanks to Him for having afflicted you will be greater than your prayers were to remove the affliction. In comparison with this misfortune all the other benefits you have received from Him will appear to have been very slight favors indeed. You have always regarded the temporal blessings He has hitherto showered on you and your family as the effects of His goodness towards you, but now you will see clearly and realize to the depths of your being that He has never loved you so much as when He took away all that He gave you for your prosperity, and that if He was generous in giving you a family, a good position, an income and good health, He has been over-generous in taking them all away.

I am not referring to the merit we acquire by the virtue of patience. Generally speaking, one day of adversity can be of more profit to us for our eternal salvation than years of untroubled living, whatever good use we make of the time.

It is common knowledge that prosperity has the effect of softening us. When a man is materially well off and content with his state, it is a great deal if he takes the trouble to think of God two or three times a day. His mind is so pleasantly occupied with his worldly affairs that it is easy for him to forget all the rest. Adversity on the other hand leads us as if naturally to raise our eyes to Heaven to seek consolation in our distress.

Certainly, God can be glorified whatever condition we are in, and the life of a Christian who serves Him when fortune is favorable is most pleasing to Him. But can he please Him as much as the man who blesses Him while he is suffering? It cannot be doubted that a man who enjoys good health, position, wealth and the world's esteem, if he uses his advantages as he ought, attributing them to God and thanking Him for them, by doing so glorifies his Maker and leads a Christian life. But if Providence takes away what he has and strikes him down, and in the midst of his reverses he continues to express the same sentiments, returning the same thanks and obeying his Lord with the same promptness and submission as he did formerly, it is then that he proclaims the glory of God and the efficacy of His grace in the most convincing and striking manner.

Opportunities for acquiring merit and saving our souls

Judge then what recompense those persons will receive from Christ who have followed Him along the way of His Cross. On the judgment day we shall understand how much God has loved us by giving us the opportunities to merit so rich a reward. Then we shall reproach ourselves for complaining at what was meant to increase our happiness, for grieving when we should have been rejoicing, for doubting God's goodness when He was giving us concrete evidence of it. If such will be our feelings one day, why not anticipate them now? Why not bless God here and now for something we shall be thanking Him for everlastingly in heaven?

It is clear from this that whatever the manner of our life we should always accept adversity joyfully. If we are leading a good life adversity purifies us, makes us better and enables us to acquire greater merit. If our life is sinful it serves to bring us to repentance and obliges us to become good.

3. Recourse *to* Prayer

It is a strange fact that though Christ repeatedly and solemnly promised to answer our prayers, most Christians are continually complaining that He does not do so. We cannot account for this by saying that the reason is because of the kind of things we ask for, since He included everything in His promise — *All things whatsoever you shall ask.* Nor can we attribute it to the unworthiness of those who ask, for His promise extended to everybody without exception — *Whoever asks shall*

43

receive. Why is it then that so many prayers remain unanswered? Can it be that as most people are never satisfied, they make such excessive and impatient demands on God that they tire and annoy Him by their importunity? The case is just the opposite. The only reason why we obtain so little from God is because we ask for so little and we are not insistent enough.

Christ promised on behalf of His Father that He would give us *everything,* even the very smallest things. But He laid down an order to be observed in all that we ask, and if we do not obey this rule, we are unlikely to obtain anything. He tells us in St. Matthew: *Seek first the kingdom of God and his justice and all these things shall be given to you besides.*

To obtain what we want

We are not forbidden to wish for money, material well-being and whatever is necessary to maintain us in our position in life, but we must wish for these things in their proper order. If we want our desires in this respect to be met without fail, we must first of all ask for the larger things, so that while granting them He may also add the smaller ones.

We can take an example from the case of Solomon. God gave him the choice of whatever he desired and he asked for wisdom, which was needful for him to carry out his kingly duties. He did not ask for riches or glory, judging that if God gave him such an opportunity, he ought to make use of it to obtain the greatest advantage. His prudence gained for him both what he asked for and what he did not ask for. *Because thou hast asked this thing, and hast not asked for thyself long life or riches . . . behold I have done for thee according to thy words* –I will willingly grant you wisdom because you have asked me for it, but I will give you long life, honor and riches as well because you did not ask for any of them — *Yea, and the things also which thou didst not ask, to wit, riches and glory.*

If then this is the order God observes in the distribution of His benefits, we must not be surprised if our prayers have so far been unsuccessful. I confess that I am often moved to pity when I see the eagerness of some people in giving alms, making vows of pilgrimage and fasting, or having Masses said for the success of their temporal affairs. I am afraid the prayers they say and get said are of little use. They should make their offerings and vow their pilgrimages to obtain from God the amendment of their lives, the gift of Christian patience, contempt for the things of the world and detachment from creatures. Then afterwards they could pray for return of health or success in business. God would then answer these prayers, or rather He would anticipate them; it would be enough to know their desires for Him to fulfil them.

Until we have obtained these first graces, anything else may be harmful to us and, in fact, usually is so. That is the reason why we are refused. We murmur and accuse God of not keeping His promises. But our God is a Father of kindness who prefers to put up with our complaints and criticisms rather than stop them by gifts which would be fatal to us.

To be delivered from evil

What has been said of benefits can also be said of the ills from which we wish to be delivered. I do not desire wealth, a person will say, but I would be satisfied with not having to suffer hardship. I leave fame and reputation to those who want it, but I would like at least not to be an object of scorn. I can do without pleasures, but I cannot support pain; I have prayed and begged God to lessen it but He will not hear me. It is not surprising. You have secret ills far greater than the ills you complain of, but you do not ask Him to deliver you from them. If for this purpose you had said half the prayers you have said to be healed from your outward ills, God would have delivered you from both a long time since. Poverty serves to keep you humble while your nature is proud, the scorn of the world to free you from your attachment to it, illness to keep you from the pleasure-seeking which would be your ruin. It would be hating you, not loving you, to take away your cross before giving you the virtues you lack. If God found some desire in you for these virtues, He would give you them without delay, and it would be unnecessary for you to ask for the other things.

We do not ask enough

It is clear then that we do not receive anything because we do not ask enough. God could not give us little, He could not restrict His liberality to small things without doing us grave harm. Do not misunderstand me. I am not saying that we offend God if we ask for temporal benefits or to be freed from misfortune. Obviously, prayers of this kind can rightly be addressed to Him by making the condition that they are not contrary to His glory or our eternal salvation. But as it is hardly likely that it would redound to His glory for Him to answer them, or to our advantage to have them answered if our wishes end there, it must be repeated that as long as we are content with little, we run the risk of obtaining nothing.

Let me show you a good way to ask for happiness even in this world. It is a way that will oblige God to listen to you. Say to him earnestly: Either give me so much money that my heart will be satisfied, or inspire me with such contempt for it that I no longer want it.

Either free me from poverty, or make it so pleasant for me that I would not exchange it for all the wealth in the world. Either take away my suffering, or – which would be to your greater glory – change it into delight for me, and instead of causing me affliction, let it become a source of joy. You can take away the burden of my cross, or you can leave it with me without my feeling its weight. You can extinguish the fire that burns me, or you can let it burn in such a way that it refreshes me as it did the three youths in the fiery furnace. I ask you for either one thing or the other. What does it matter in what way I am happy? If I am happy through the possession of worldly goods, it is you I have to thank. If I am happy when deprived of them, it gives you greater glory and my thanks are all the greater.

This is the kind of prayer worthy of being offered to God by a true Christian. When you pray in this way, do you know what the effect of your prayers will be? First, you will be satisfied whatever happens; and what else do those who most desire this world's goods want except to be satisfied? Secondly, you will not only obtain without fail one of the two things you have asked for but, as a rule, you will obtain both of them. God will give you the enjoyment of wealth, and so that you may possess it without the danger of becoming attached to it, He will inspire you at the same time with contempt for it. He will put an end to your sufferings and even more He will leave you with a desire for them which will give you all the merit of patience without having to suffer. In a word He will make you happy here and now, and lest your happiness should do you harm, He will let you know and feel the emptiness of it. Can one ask for anything better? But if such a great blessing is well worth being asked for, remember that still more is it worth being asked for with insistence. For the reason why we obtain little is not only because we ask for little but still more because, whether we ask a little or we ask a lot, we do not ask often enough.

Perseverance in Prayer

If you want all your prayers to be answered without fail and oblige God to meet all your wishes, the first thing is never to stop praying. Those who get tired after praying for a time are lacking in either humility or confidence, and so do not deserve to be heard. You would think that they expected their requests to be obeyed at once as if they were orders. Surely, we know that God resists the proud and shows His favors to the humble. Won't our pride allow us to ask more than once for the same thing? It shows very little trust in God's goodness to give up so soon and take a delay for an absolute refusal.

Once we have really understood just how far God's goodness extends, we can never believe that we have been refused or that He wishes to deprive us of hope. Rather, the more He makes us keep on asking for something we want, the more confident we should feel that we shall eventually obtain it. We can begin to doubt that our prayer has been heard only when we notice we have stopped praying. If after a year we find that our prayer is as fervent as it was at the beginning, then we need not doubt about the success of our efforts, and instead of losing courage after so long a delay, we should rejoice because we can be certain that our desires will be all the more fully satisfied for the length of time we have prayed. If our first attempts had been quite useless, we would not have repeated them so often and we would have lost hope; but as we have kept on in spite of this, there is good reason to believe we shall be liberally rewarded.

In fact, it took St. Monica sixteen years to obtain the conversion of Augustine, but the conversion was entire and far beyond what she had prayed for. Her desire was that her son's incontinence might be checked by marriage, and instead she had the joy of seeing him embrace a life of holy chastity. She had only wanted him to be baptized and become a Christian, and she saw him a bishop. She asked God to turn him aside from heresy, and God made him a pillar of the Church and its champion against heretics. Think what would have happened had she given up hope after a couple of years, after ten or twelve years, when her prayers appeared to obtain no result and her son grew worse instead of better, adding avarice and ambition to the wildness of his life and sinking further and further into error. She would have wronged her son, thrown away her own happiness, and deprived the world of one of the greatest Christian thinkers.

Obstinate Trust

As a final word I address myself to those faithful souls kneeling in prayer before the altar and asking God for the graces He is so pleased to hear us asking for. You who are happy that God has shown you the vanity of the world, you who groan under the yoke of your passions and beg to be delivered from them, you who burn with desire to love God and

47

serve Him as He would be served, you who intercede with God for the sake of one who is dear to you, do not grow weary of asking, be steadfast and tireless in your demands. If you are refused today, tomorrow you will obtain everything; if this year brings nothing, the next will bring you abundance. Never think your efforts are wasted. Your every word is numbered and what you receive will be in the measure of the time you have spent asking. Your treasure is piling up and suddenly one day it will overflow to an extent beyond your dreams.

Consider the workings of Divine Providence and think that the refusal you meet with now is only God's stratagem to increase your fervor. Remember how He acted towards the Canaanite woman, treating her harshly and refusing to see or listen to her. He seemed to be irritated by her importunity, but in reality He admired it and was delighted with her trust and humility, and for that reason He repulsed her. With what tenderness does He repulse those whom He most wishes to be indulgent to, hiding His clemency under the mask of cruelty! Take care not to be deceived by it. The more He seems to be unwilling, the more you must insist.

Do as the woman of Canaan, use against Him the very arguments He may have for refusing you. It is true that to hear me, you should say to Him, would be to give the bread of the children to dogs. I do not deserve the grace I ask, but I do not ask You to give me what I deserve; I ask it through the merits of my Redeemer. You ought to think more of Your promises than of my unworthiness, and You will be unjust to Yourself if You give me only what I deserve. If I were worthier of Your benefits it would be less to Your glory to give me them. It is unjust to grant favors to a sinner, but I do not appeal to Your justice but to Your mercy.

Do not lose courage when you have begun so well to struggle with God. Do not give Him a moment's rest. He loves the violence of your attack and wants to be overcome by you. Make importunity your watchword, let persistence be a miracle in you. Compel God to throw off the mask and say to you with admiration *'Great is thy faith, be it done as thou wishest.* I can no longer resist you, you shall have what you desire, in this life and the next.'

Exercise *in* Conformity *to* Divine Providence

1. Act *of* Faith, Hope *and* Charity
2. Act *of* Filial Submission *to* Providence
3. Usefulness *of* This Exercise

The practice of this exercise is of great importance because of the advantages it always confers on those who undertake it devoutly.

1. Act *of* Faith, Hope *and* Charity

First make an act of faith in God's Providence. Meditate well on the truth that God's continual care extends not only to all things in general but to each particular thing, and especially to ourselves, our souls and bodies, and everything that concerns us. Nothing escapes His loving watchfulness – our work, our daily needs, our health as well as our infirmities, our life and our death, even the smallest hair on our head which cannot fall without His permission.

After this act of faith, make an act of hope. Excite in yourself a firm trust that God will provide for all you need, will direct and protect you with more than a father's love and vigilance, and guide you in such a way that, whatever happens, if you submit to Him everything will turn out for your happiness and advantage, even the things that may seem quite the opposite.

To these two an act of charity should be added. Show your deep love and attachment for Divine Providence as a child shows for its mother by taking refuge in her arms. Say how highly you esteem all His intentions, however hidden they may be, in the knowledge that they spring from an infinite wisdom which cannot make a mistake and supreme goodness which can wish only the perfection of His creatures. Determine that this feeling will have a practical result in making you ready to speak out in defense of Providence whenever you hear it denied or criticized.

2. Act *of* Filial Submission *to* Providence

After repeating these acts several times with fervor, commit your soul lovingly to Divine Providence as a child rests and sleeps in its mother's arms. Make your own the words of David: *I will lie down and sleep in peace, for thou alone, O Lord, hast established me in hope.*[78] Or again in the words of the psalm:

> *The Lord is my shepherd; I shall not want.*
> *In verdant pastures he gives me repose;*
> *Beside restful waters he leads me; he refreshes my soul.*
> *He guides me in right paths for his name's sake.*
> *Even though I walk in the dark valley*
> *I fear no evil; for you are at my side*
> *With your rod and your staff that give me courage.*
> *You spread the table before me in the sight of my foes;*
> *You anoint my head with oil; my cup overflows.*
> *Only goodness and kindness follow me all the days of my life;*
> *And I shall dwell in the house of the Lord*
> *For years to come.*[79]

Filled with the joy these consoling words inspire, the soul can trustfully accept from Divine Providence whatever happens now or in the future with tranquility and peace of mind. Its happiness is that of a child who feels protected and secure. Not that it lives in idle expectation of what it needs or neglects to occupy itself with the affairs of daily life. On the contrary it does all in its power and employs all its faculties in attending to them well. But what it does it does under God's guidance and regards its own judgment as entirely subject to God's. It freely entrusts everything to His governance without expecting any other result from its actions but what is in accordance with His will.

3. Usefulness *of* This Exercise

What honor and glory is given to God by the soul that acts thus!

It is a great glory for Him to have a creature so attached to His Providence, so dependent on Him, full of such firm hope and peace of mind in the expectation of what He will send. His concern for such a one is redoubled, He watches over the slightest things that are of interest to him and inspires those who are over him to act prudently; and if for any reason they try to act in a manner harmful to him, He prevents them in the hidden ways of His Providence from carrying out their designs and compels them to do only what is to his advantage.

---

[78] Ps. 4:9   [79] id. 22:1-6

Thus, the Lord keeps those who love him.[80] If the Scriptures speak of God as having eyes, it is in order to watch over them; as having ears, to hear them; as having hands, to defend them. And those who touch them, touch the apple of His eye. *I shall carry you in my arms,* He says by the mouth of the prophet Isaias, *I shall caress you upon my knees. As one whom his mother caresses, so will I comfort you*[81]-And in Osee: *I was like a foster father to Ephraim, I carried them in my arms.*[82] Long before Moses had said: *In the desert the Lord your God carried you, as a man carries his child, all along your journey until you arrived at this place.*[83] Again God says in Isaias: *You shall be nursed with the breasts of kings, and you shall know that I am the Lord your Savior and your Redeemer.*[84]

In the person of Noah, we can find a figure of the happiness of the man who throws himself entirely upon God. While the floodgates of heaven were opened and the world was laid in ruin Noah was safe and at peace in the ark because God was guiding him. Others remained at the mercy of the waters, losing all they had, their families, their lives. Thus, the man who entrusts himself to Providence, lets God be the pilot of his bark, floats tranquilly on the ocean of life in the midst of storm and tempest, while those who try to guide themselves are in continual unrest, and their only pilot being their own inconstant will, they are tossed about by sea and wind until they end in shipwreck.

Let us then trust ourselves entirely to God and His Providence and leave Him complete power to order our lives, turning to Him lovingly in every need and awaiting His help without anxiety. Leave everything to Him and He will provide us with everything, at the time and in the place and in the manner best suited. He will lead us on our way to that happiness and peace of mind for which we are destined in this life as a foretaste of the everlasting happiness we have been promised.

---

[80] *Ps. 144:20*
[81] *Is. 66:12-13*
[82] *Osee 11:3*
[83] *Deut. 1:31*
[84] *Is. 60:16*

Promise Date: 26-OCT-23 (THU) Promise Date: 26-OCT-23 (THU)

761974LV00009B/80
10PING-SS:BW
CASE

761974LVX00140B - 761974LVX00146B [7 : 11]

761974LV00009B

BOOK
CRMGRWD_RY   CONTAINS: MONO

Department   Operator's Name (Please print)

Printing _____

Binding _____

Cutting _____

Shipping _____

Batch Location _____

761974LV

Promise Date: 26-OCT-23 (T